THE
NORMANS

Brenda Williams

revised by
Gill Knappe

The buildings of Battle Abbey:
the site of the Battle of Hastings.

Eynt Edward par la grce deu vist le sour de pal

The Last Anglo-Saxon King

ABOVE: This medieval painting shows Edward the Confessor seated at a banquet.

THE YEAR OF 1066 FOUND ENGLAND IN CRISIS. Even before the Normans landed on British shores, the English monarchy was in unsteady hands, with multiple claimants vying for an increasingly fractured country.

Edward the Confessor

Edward ruled from 1042–66. Interested in art and religion, his devotion led him to rebuild Westminster Abbey and earned him his title: the Confessor. Half Norman, and exiled in Normandy for many years, he preferred Norman ways. But he was a weak man, and having returned from exile found himself dominated by Earl Godwin and his son Harold. When, to counter them, the king appointed officials from Normandy, he roused resentment among the mainly Anglo-Scandinavian aristocracy, who kept close links with rulers in the Viking homelands.

Three claimants

Edward the Confessor's reign was largely peaceful but, despite his marriage to Edith, daughter of Earl Godwin, he failed to produce an heir. As the king's life drew to a close, three claimants were clawing for the throne: Duke William of Normandy; Harald Hardrada, King of Norway; and Harold Godwinson of Wessex, son of the politically acute Earl Godwin.

Edward's Norman allies had urged him to make William his heir and the duke was quick to put forward his claim to the English Crown with the backing of the Pope in Rome. However, in England, both the Witan (king's noble council) and the Church supported Edward's brother-in-law, the soldierly and popular Harold Godwinson.

Death of a king

Born in 1022, Harold had been supreme in the council since his father's death in 1053. It was he that Edward the Confessor, on his deathbed, named as his successor, and he was duly crowned King Harold II. It is possible that Harold was crowned in Westminster Abbey, that awe-inspiring place that also saw the burial of Edward the Confessor. If so, so began the tradition of funerals and coronations at Westminster Abbey.

BELOW: The funeral of Edward the Confessor, depicted in the Bayeux Tapestry. His masterpiece, Westminster Abbey, can be seen to the left.

ABOVE: A 13th-century imagining of the Battle of Hastings; Duke William of Normandy stabs King Harold of England as they fight on horseback.

The Conquerors Come

T HE NEW KING, HAROLD II, didn't offer any stability to the kingdom. England was still ripe for the conquest, with claimants in both Scandinavia and Normandy ready to seize its throne.

Normandy, founded by the Vikings in 911, was already a kingdom of conquerors. In the first half of the 11th century, they had attacked Sicily, southern Italy and parts of Byzantium. By 1130, as well as England, the Normans also ruled these lands, as well as huge sections of the North African coastline.

One hundred and fifty years after the foundation of the Norman peoples, an army of descendants of these 'Northmen' prepared to cross the Channel and invade the bigger, richer kingdom of the English. The Norman leader, Duke William, considered the land rightfully his, promised both by his childless kinsman, Edward the Confessor, and by Harold Godwinson.

ABOVE: A map depicting the routes of the various military forces during the turbulent year of 1066.

Attack from the north

Expecting William's reaction to his coronation, Harold deployed forces on the south coast, but found himself instead facing invasion from Scandinavia. This was led by the King of Norway, Harald Hardrada, and Harold's own wayward brother, Tostig. They landed in northern England. Marching swiftly north, on 25 September 1066, Harold won a famous victory at Stamford Bridge, near York: both Harald Hardrada and Tostig were killed.

Three days later, a fleet of 700 Norman ships landed at Pevensey on the Sussex coast. King Harold wheeled south, spurning delay for reinforcements in favour of speed and surprise.

The Battle of Hastings

William's army was waiting. Saxon England fought for its life that autumn Saturday on Senlac Hill. Its foot soldiers stood firm against archers and cavalry, but broke ranks to chase fleeing Normans and were cut to pieces. According to the Norman monk-historian Ordericus Vitalis, the battle was fought 'with the greatest fury' from nine in the morning until the evening. King Harold II died at dusk at the foot of his royal standard; his bodyguard, brandishing battleaxes, fought to the last man.

Harold's death at the Battle of Hastings – just nine months after his coronation – and that of his brothers Leofwin and Girth meant that after 500 years of Saxon rule in England invading Norsemen had finally triumphed, allowing William to take the Crown and earn his title: the Conqueror.

THE BAYEUX TAPESTRY

The Bayeux Tapestry is believed to have been made in England in Canterbury, Kent, commissioned in the 1070s by Bishop Odo of Bayeux, half-brother of William the Conqueror.

Recounting King William I's conquest on 14 October 1066, the artwork consists of a series of panels, whose story starts with Harold's visit to Normandy, where he swears to uphold William's claim to the English throne. Harold insisted the oath was made under duress as a prisoner. The famous scene of a warrior struck in the eye with an arrow has often been taken as depicting Harold receiving his death wound. The tapestry also gives an important historical insight into how the Normans lived, fought and built castles, with the early castle at Hastings shown under construction.

Today the Bayeux Tapestry is preserved and displayed in the Bayeux Museum in Normandy, France.

Rule of the Sword

BORN IN 1028, WILLIAM WAS AN ILLEGITIMATE SON of Duke Robert I of Normandy. William, who took the title after his father's death in 1035, grew to become a vigorous soldier with a fierce will, physical strength and disciplined habits. His wife, Matilda, bore him several children and acted as regent in Normandy when her husband set off to conquer England.

William was determined to bend England to his will. To force its surrender he marched his troops around London, slaughtering and burning wherever he met resistance. One by one the cities, churchmen and nobles submitted to their new master. On Christmas Day 1066, the Conqueror was crowned at Westminster Abbey.

A chaotic coronation

It was Edward the Confessor who built the new abbey at Westminster, consecrated on 28 December 1065, just days before he died. Edward, the only English monarch to have been canonized, was the first sovereign to be enshrined here, so beginning a long tradition of royal burials and memorials at the abbey.

When William the Conqueror was crowned at Westminster Abbey in 1066 another tradition began, as this has been the site for coronations of English monarchs ever since. However, his ceremony did not go smoothly: shouts of acclaim from the English-speaking members of the congregation were misinterpreted by the French-speaking guards as a protest, and they set fire to nearby houses in retaliation. Although the ceremony

continued, panicked guests left the smoke-filled abbey, the clergy were terrified and King William 'was trembling violently'.

Crushing the rebels

William soon departed for Normandy, leaving his half-brother Odo, Bishop of Bayeux, to consolidate the work of conquest. In late 1067 William was back to crush a revolt at Exeter and in 1069 savagely punished a great northern rebellion. Rebels who had sacked Peterborough Abbey with Hereward the Wake were ruthlessly hunted down but Edric the Wild, leader of resistance on the Welsh borders, was pardoned. Norman retribution was apparently not always merciless. Having completed his conquest of England, William then advanced on Scotland to gain the

submission of its king, Malcolm Canmore, in 1072. King Malcolm III acknowledged this, but thereafter proceeded to continue to raid England.

Steadily but remorselessly, French-speaking Normans spread through England's government and Church. They already had its land. English land was William's own battle spoil, the reward he shared out to the military chiefs who had helped him win it. They held it as his vassals, swearing allegiance and fighting for him when called. Land-holding was the basis of Norman feudalism. The king's land was let to barons; barons let land to knights and freemen; they in turn let land to peasants, who worked the lord's land and their own. By the time William ordered the Domesday survey of his kingdom in 1085, some 200 Normans had replaced over 4,000 Saxon landlords.

THE DOMESDAY BOOK

William the Conqueror made only four visits to England between 1072 and 1087. The last occasion was noteworthy for the most astonishing feat of Norman bureaucracy – William's survey of the kingdom, known as the Domesday Book and so-called because, like the Day of Judgement (Day of Doom), no one could escape its scrutiny.

In 1086 William I sent officials to survey land resources in England. Nothing like it had been attempted before. County by county, land-holdings were listed, described and assessed for tax and value, with comparisons drawn between 1066 and 1086. The officials heard evidence sworn in court by juries of priests, reeves and six men from each village. A typical entry reads: 'In Wallington, Fulco holds of Gilbert 3 hides and 40 acres of land. There is land for five ploughs … There is pasture for beasts and wood for hedges … Altogether it is worth 50s [shillings]. When he received it, 30s. At the time of King Edward, 100s.'

The Domesday Book remains an invaluable historical record, giving a fascinating snapshot of the land the Normans found. It proved as important as Norman castles in relation to subduing English independence.

ABOVE: Norman knights, riding straight-legged, charging into battle with the lance held steady beneath the arm.

RETVR:CASTELLVM:AT·HESTENGA CEASTRA

Church and Castle

ABOVE: A scene from the Bayeux Tapestry, depicting the building of the mound for the castle at Hastings.

THE SAXONS HAD SETTLED IN BRITAIN to farm, but the Normans came to rule. The *Anglo-Saxon Chronicle* reported that the Normans 'built castles far and wide throughout the land'. With a few exceptions, such fortresses were a new phenomenon in England.

As soon as William became ruler, fortifications were started at Pevensey, Hastings, Dover, London and Winchester, and before long a string of castles stretched from Warwick to York, dominating the Midlands, with more in Eastern England in Lincoln, Huntingdon and Cambridge.

Around 200 castles were built in the 35 years following the Norman conquest. Early wooden buildings were soon replaced by massive castles of stone, among them the Tower of London. Under Norman rule, London became the undisputed capital of England.

A small army of occupation kept control of the surrounding area from the castles, which acted as barracks, watchtowers, forts and administrative headquarters, commanding the landscape as a stark reminder of William's brooding power. From these symbols of Norman domination, cavalry patrols rode out to stifle the uprisings and invasions that continued for five years. Though cowed, the Saxons were not yet quelled.

A scholarly kingdom

William, a good churchman, had seized England with the Pope's blessing. The Conqueror was proud of the monasteries he had founded: 'While I was duke, seventeen abbeys of monks and six of nuns were built … These are the fortresses by which Normandy is guarded.' Famed for their learning, these establishments attracted the Italian scholars Lanfranc and Anselm, who were in turn to be made Archbishop of Canterbury by William and his successor.

William founded his first English abbey at Battle, on the site of his victory. He sought to order the English Church as he had its government, using energetic scholars, administrators, builders and businessmen from Normandy to modernize a Church whose long-venerated Saxon saints they viewed as 'rustic', and whose

MOTTE AND BAILEY CASTLES
Norman castles were of the motte and bailey design. An area of land (the bailey) was surround by a ditch and bank, topped by a palisade (wooden fence). Within the bailey, or beside it, was a steep-sided mound (the motte) on top of which stood a wooden tower or donjon (keep), the residence of the castle owner. Such castles could be built in a week using forced labour.

'While I was duke, seventeen abbeys of monks and six of nuns were built … These are the fortresses by which Normandy is guarded.'

abbots they thought 'uncultured idiots'. Lanfranc organized dioceses and cathedral chapters, developed separate Church courts and Church law. He also tried to make a priest's blessing requisite for lawful marriage and to impose celibacy on the priesthood.

Places of God

The Normans built churches as enthusiastically as they built castles, replacing almost every major foundation in England within decades. Their early Romanesque style – thick, monumental, with huge stone columns and heavy, rounded arches – mirrors the builders' qualities of strength, energy, confidence and endurance. The grandest examples, in the cathedrals at Durham, Ely, Norwich and the great abbey churches of Gloucester and Tewkesbury, have aisles, galleries and arcades flanking extremely long naves. Saxons provided the labour but stonemasons, craftsmen and even the stone were imported from Normandy for the work. This was organized by monks such as Bishop Gundulf of Rochester, who rebuilt the

DOVER CASTLE

Dover Castle in Kent commands a perfect position over the sea crossing between England and France. Immediately after defeating Harold, William the Conqueror strengthened the defences of the fortress, replacing an earlier wooden structure on the old Saxon-Roman fort site. Particularly significant was its massive Norman keep: the weight of its immense towers, 30 metres (98 feet) square and with walls up to 7 metres (23 feet) thick, meant that they could be built only on very solid mounds (ideally rock). Castle walls often contained small rooms (used as sleeping quarters, latrines, stores and guardrooms). At Dover, the outer ring wall was protected by crenellations (battlements), and the gateway was defended by flanking towers. Dover's keep had four storeys, the royal quarters being on the second floor. Entrances were normally on the first floor, reached by an external staircase, and the only windows were in the upper floors.

cathedral and castle there, and is also credited with designing the White Tower of the Tower of London.

Bishops could wield as much power as barons. Some, like Odo, were barons in their own right, but they also held the Church's lands in trust from the king, swearing fealty and rendering knight service for it. William, however, insisted on mastery of his newly-won kingdom. He refused to do homage to the Pope for it, further declaring that no Pope was to be recognized in England without the king's sanction.

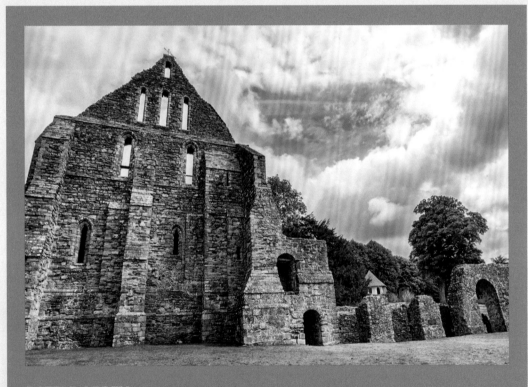

BATTLE ABBEY

Speaking before the Battle of Hastings, the confident Duke William of Normandy vowed to build 'a fitting monastery, with a worthy liberty' on the site of the impending attack 'for the salvation of all, and especially for those who fall here … Let it be an atonement: a haven for all as free as the one I conquer for myself.'

True to his word, William built the Benedictine Battle Abbey on the site where so much blood was shed on that day in 1066, and legend has it that the high altar marked the spot where King Harold was killed. But not only was the monastery a symbol of the Conqueror's penance, it also represented his power.

The Law of the Land

WILLIAM THE CONQUEROR granted land units (fiefs) shrewdly, allocating half of all farmland to the nobles, and a quarter to the Church. The rest he kept for himself. Nobles governed their estates, or manors, for the king from their castles or fortified manor houses. When a noble died, his son paid a tax to the king and asked permission to inherit the estate.

No castle could be built without the king's approval and no baron could keep a private army. In this way William sought to prevent wars in England like those waged between nobles in Normandy. To counterbalance the power of individual barons over their local area, he retained the Saxon system of sheriffs acting on the king's behalf.

William began by confirming the laws of Edward the Confessor. He retained Saxon forms of government, and even tried to learn English, but by the end of his reign the Norman flair for adaptation had produced a Normanized administration run by officials with such titles as steward, butler, chamberlain, constable, marshal and chancellor. The chancellor headed the scriptorium, the department issuing royal commands or writs, which were produced at first in English but later in Latin. The Normans themselves spoke Norman French.

LEFT: A penny coin depicting William the Conqueror.

ABOVE: William the Conqueror granting a charter to the City of London. Illustration from Cassell's *History of England*, 1912.

Death of the Conqueror

B Y 1086 WILLIAM THE CONQUEROR was back in Normandy. Although he cut a formidable figure he was, by now, considerably overweight. In 1087 he was confined to bed, possibly with a stomach complaint, but in July of that year was roused into action and raised an army when the garrison of the French fortress of Mantes made a raid into Normandy. One account reports that while seizing Mantes William was injured when his horse jumped a ditch and the pommel of the saddle was forced into the king's stomach. Another report claims King William suffered heat exhaustion during the offensive. Whatever the cause of the problem, the ailing king was taken to the church of Saint Gervase in Rouen where, on 9 September 1087, he died. After a funeral service at St Gervase, William's body was taken for burial at a church he had founded in 1063: the Abbey of Saint-Étienne in Caen, Normandy.

BELOW: William I hunting, from a 14th-century manuscript. He created the New Forest as a royal hunting ground.

Inheritance troubles

The Conqueror left three sons and two dominions. Normandy was given to the eldest son, Robert; England to William, called 'Rufus'

('red') because of his fair hair and florid complexion; the third son, Henry, was left a fortune in silver. The division precipitated a determined struggle between them for each other's land.

Robert, whose lack of height gave him the name Curthose ('Short leggings'), was reputedly lazy and dissolute and his dukedom soon descended into lawlessness. Rufus, by contrast, was as capable and determinedly ruthless as his father. He twice invaded Normandy, whereupon Robert pawned him the duchy in order to join the First Crusade. Barons with lands in both Normandy and England had sworn fealty to each of the Conqueror's sons and were forced to break faith with one or the other when fighting broke out.

The Conqueror's half-brother Odo supported Robert; Lanfranc and the Saxons of England supported Rufus. Odo was banished and joined Robert on the First Crusade (1095–99) – the first of a number of crusades which aimed to recapture the Holy Land, called for by Pope Urban II in 1095 – but he died on the way and was buried at Palermo in Sicily.

ABOVE: The tomb of William the Conqueror at the Abbey of Saint-Étienne in Normandy.

Brothers in Arms

KING WILLIAM II'S STRENGTH AND GIRTH marked him out as the son of the Conqueror. Born in 1056, he was reckless, greedy and opportunistic, qualities which won him approval from his knights but earned the displeasure of monks who condemned with distaste the fashions of his court – long hair, pointed shoes and effeminate behaviour.

William Rufus, crowned soon after his father's death, continued the Conqueror's task of crushing rebellion amongst the English while extending Norman authority into South Wales and northern England, settling Cumberland with southern peasants and

NORMAN KNIGHTS

Normans, like their Viking ancestors, were skilled horsemen who relished the battlefield and the hunting forest. Their warhorse was the destrier, ridden high in a built-up saddle by knights wearing the hauberk, a knee-length shirt of mail, and a conical helmet with a projecting nosepiece protecting the head. A long, kite-shaped shield of leather, stretched on a wooden frame, covered the body.

Knights charged almost standing in their long stirrups, a lance ready to thrust at the enemy. In hand-to-hand fighting they slashed with a broad-bladed sword, a valuable possession often handed down through the generations. Spears were also a choice but fighting bishops like Odo wielded the mace, an iron club that felled the enemy yet met Church rule that priests cause no bloodshed.

refortifying Carlisle, previously under Scottish control. One of many raids by the Scots resulted, in 1093, in the death of King Malcolm, after which Rufus nominated each of Malcolm's three sons to the Scottish throne in turn, as his vassals.

William II cared little for the Church. But, having appointed Anselm as Archbishop of Canterbury, the king became embroiled in the Europe-wide tussle between Church and state in the matter of investing priests. He kept Church appointments vacant to appropriate the revenue for himself.

A hunting 'accident'

Like their father, William I's sons were enthusiast huntsmen. The Conqueror had turned great tracts of land into royal hunting

BELOW: King William II, also known as William Rufus, on his throne wounded by an arrow, c.1307-27.

19

parks, displacing inhabitants and imposing harsh penalties on those who poached his deer and wild boar. But hunting was also dangerous. In August 1100, as his brother Robert Curthose was returning a hero from the Crusades, William Rufus was killed in the New Forest, shot in the back, apparently by a stray arrow. The man blamed for the accident, Walter Tirel, fled abroad. The king's other brother, Henry, also hunting that day, rushed immediately to Winchester where he seized the treasury. Rufus's body was left for peasants to take by cart to Winchester Cathedral.

William Rufus had never married. Three days after his death, Henry was crowned King of England. There is no proof that he had anything to do with Rufus's mysterious end, but he undoubtedly profited from it.

WINCHESTER CATHEDRAL

William the Conqueror installed the French-born Bishop Walkelin at Winchester and in 1079 work started on a new church, in the Norman Romanesque style, to replace the Old Minster. The cathedrals and abbeys of Norman England were built on a grander scale than their Norman counterparts and the nave at Winchester stretched an impressive 81 metres (266 feet),

making it the longest in Europe. On 15 July 1093, the new cathedral was consecrated.

William Rufus's body was buried beneath the tower of Winchester Cathedral, the authorities being reluctant to grant Church rites. The tower collapsed in 1107, and the king's bones are believed to lie in a mortuary chest which can be seen in the cathedral.

Henry's Rule

O N WILLIAM RUFUS'S DEATH HIS ELDER BROTHER, Robert Curthose, returned from the Crusades with money to redeem his dukedom but Henry, William's younger brother, had no intention of letting him. Following a failed invasion of England in 1101, Robert renounced his claim in favour of a pension. Henry then landed in France, defeated and captured his brother at Tinchebrai in 1106 and kept him prisoner. He died at Cardiff Castle in 1134, aged 80, and was buried in the abbey church at Gloucester (now Gloucester Cathedral). England and Normandy had a single ruler once more.

A stable kingdom

The Norman kingdom was at its largest and most powerful under Henry I, the most able and ruthless ruler amongst the Conqueror's sons. 'False-coiners' (counterfeiters) were mutilated on his orders to discourage others from following their example.

Welsh and Scottish kings remained Henry's vassals. Promising good government, he issued a charter of liberties and extended his father's administrative reforms. He issued sealed writs, employed travelling justices for matters of royal concern, and appointed a

ABOVE: The great seal of Henry I as depicted in a 19th-century engraving.

justiciar as a regent when he was absent in Normandy. Trade and towns grew, especially London, which was granted a charter allowing it to elect its own justices and collect its own customs duties. Henry also made amends with Anselm and the Church, keeping the homage of the bishops but giving way on the king's right to the spiritual investiture of priests.

Spirituality and learning

Continuing Norman support for monastic reform, Henry received Cistercian monks to England, where they founded Rievaulx and Fountains abbeys in Yorkshire and raised the sheep on which England's future prosperity would be built. The Church also

FOUNTAINS ABBEY

In 1132 Fountains Abbey was founded by 13 Benedictine monks who, disillusioned with the extravagant lifestyle of the monks at St Mary's in York, sought a simpler and more devout life elsewhere. They were admitted to the austere Cistercian order and Fountains became the second Cistercian abbey in North Yorkshire, after Rievaulx.

educated those entering the priesthood, government or law, all of which used Latin, although in the late 11th century a certain Master Theobald of Étampes was instructing between 60 and 100 students at Oxford.

Family alliances

Henry excelled at diplomatic marriage, disposing his 21 illegitimate children (a record for an English king) to produce a ring of favourable friendships. He himself had chosen to marry Matilda of Scotland (originally christened Edith). She was the daughter of King Malcolm III of Scotland and Queen Margaret, the great-granddaughter of the Saxon king AEthelred II 'The Unready'.

HENRY'S NIGHTMARE

When he ascended the throne Henry I vowed to abolish injustice and uphold good laws, but failed to keep his promise. In the *Chronicon ex chronicis*, credited to monk and chronicler John of Worcester, it is claimed that as a result of his broken pledge King Henry was tormented by nightmares. The 'three orders' of Norman society – those who prayed, those who fought and those who laboured – appeared in the king's dream in protest against high taxes. Soon after, he was caught in a storm at sea and promised not to collect Danegeld (a tax to raise funds for protection against Danish invaders) for seven years and to preserve justice.

Matilda

ONE OF HENRY'S TRIUMPHS had been to marry his 11-year-old daughter Matilda to the German (Holy Roman) Emperor in 1114. A huge dowry of silver brought her the title of Empress that she used all her life. However it was Henry's son William – 18 months younger than Matilda – who carried the king's hopes for succession. When 17-year-old William drowned in 1120 it was a personal and dynastic disaster for Henry.

A female heir

Following the sinking of the *Blanche-Nef* Henry I had no more sons. When the nearest male heir, Robert's son William Clito, was killed in 1128, Henry had already fixed his ambitions on his eldest daughter, Matilda. After her husband's death in 1125 she returned to England, where Henry made his barons swear allegiance to her as heir, in association with 'her lawful husband, should she have one'. And Matilda soon did. He was Geoffrey, Count of Anjou, whom she married in 1128 to disrupt Anjou's alliance with the King of France. She was 26 and he was just 15. King Henry I was delighted to have two grandsons during his lifetime: Henry in 1133 and Geoffrey a year later.

ABOVE: A 15th-century depiction of Matilda, daughter of Henry I.

'Each of his triumphs only made him worry lest he lose what he had gained; therefore though he seemed to be the most fortunate of kings, he was in truth the most miserable.'

THE CHRONICLER HENRY OF HUNTINGDON ON HENRY I

ABOVE: A portrait of Geoffrey, Count of Anjou. Nicknamed Plantagenet, he was married to Matilda in 1128 at the age of 15.

THE WHITE SHIP TRAGEDY

King Henry I's first-born son, Duke William of Normandy, was on board the *Blanche-Nef*, part of the royal fleet, with other members of the Anglo-Norman court one cold November night in 1120. The ship, on which nearly everyone aboard was drunk, had just set sail for England when it struck a rock off the Normandy coast. Although the heir to the English throne found safety in a dinghy, on hearing the cries of one of his half-sisters he turned back to rescue her. The dinghy capsized and William was drowned.

Of 200 aboard the ship, just one survived.

Although their marriage was stormy, Matilda bore her husband a third son, William, in 1136.

The death of the king

The Norman nobles, resistant at the prospect of a woman as their liege lord, were forced to renew allegiance to Matilda, while the heiress and her husband quarrelled between themselves and with King Henry, demanding land, money and castles in characteristic Norman style. Henry himself lived most of the time near his grandchildren in France, where in 1135 he fell ill and died at a hunting lodge, traditionally reported as the result of a meal of lampreys, but possibly of a heart attack.

Matilda was met as an invader in Normandy by the nobles who owed her homage. While the barons decided what to do next, her cousin Stephen took action. Stephen of Blois, son of William the Conqueror's daughter Adela, had grown up at the court of his uncle, King Henry. The king's death was Stephen's chance – and he took it.

BELOW: The ruins of Reading Abbey. Established by Henry I, he was also buried there.

King versus Empress

STEPHEN, FAVOURABLY PLACED AT BOULOGNE when Henry died, at once crossed the Channel. His lordships in Kent and Essex, on London's trade route with the Continent, helped him win the city's crucial support while Winchester, where his brother, Henry of Blois, was bishop, provided him with the treasury. Charming and affable, Stephen persuaded the Archbishop of Canterbury to crown him at Westminster on 22 December 1135.

Civil war

The barons now had either to support the enthroned King of England or risk the loss of their English lands by championing Matilda in France. Stephen needed to enforce his authority quickly. But Stephen alienated support by humiliating Roger of Salisbury, justiciar of Henry I and controller of the country's administration. Sensing an opportunity, Matilda's half-brother, Robert of Gloucester, took up her cause. When the Empress landed at Arundel in 1139, Norman England faced civil war.

The ensuing anarchy lasted until 1154. Chroniclers of the time recorded: 'It was said openly that Christ and his saints were asleep'; 'You could see villages … standing

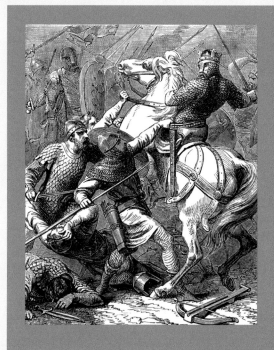

THE BATTLE OF LINCOLN

The Battle of Lincoln took place on 2 February 1141. King Stephen's men had besieged Lincoln Castle – built by William the Conqueror in 1068 – but were attacked by the forces loyal to Empress Matilda and led by Robert of Gloucester. The royal troops were outnumbered and outfought. Stephen was captured and imprisoned in Bristol Castle.

'You could see villages … standing solitary and almost empty because the peasants of both sexes and all ages were dead.'

HEDINGHAM CASTLE

The manor of Hedingham in Essex was gifted by William the Conqueror to Frenchman Aubrey de Vere in 1086. Its Great Hall was a favoured residence of King Stephen's queen, Matilda of Boulogne, who died there in 1152.

A castle hall such as that at Hedingham would have been strewn with rushes or reeds, hung with woollen embroideries, and used for eating, sleeping and business. The baronial family dined at a separate high table and retired to a private curtained area. Others dined at benches and slept on the floor.

solitary and almost empty because the peasants of both sexes and all ages were dead.' Uncurbed, the barons tasted independence, flouting royal authority, acting lawlessly, some with wanton cruelty and destruction, building unlicensed castles to house private armies. Baronial infighting, which the Norman kings had striven to prevent, now seemed set to destroy the land as towns were burned and plundered.

Neither side seemed strong enough to win. Empress Matilda's arrogance cost her the kingdom after Stephen's capture at the Battle of Lincoln.

The end of an empire

Whilst Stephen was imprisoned, Matilda planned her coronation. However, she antagonized potential support with her autocratic demands and London rose against her, as did Winchester, where Robert of Gloucester was captured and later exchanged for Stephen, who resumed the kingship.

In 1141 Matilda made her base at Oxford Castle. In the autumn of the following year Stephen attacked the town and besieged the fortress. That December, Empress Matilda escaped through the snow – legend has it dressed in white and over a frozen stream – to Abingdon. Stephen had shown his lack of Norman ruthlessness by letting Matilda slip from his grasp.

Matilda's husband, meanwhile, had been fighting his own battles for Normandy, which he finally gained in 1144. Henry I's Norman empire had fallen apart.

Matilda left England in 1148, never to return. Robert of Gloucester was dead, but the Empress's claim to the throne was kept alive by her young son Henry, who by 1150 was ruling Normandy. When Stephen's eldest son, Eustace, died plundering in East Anglia in 1153, a way opened to unite England and Normandy once more. Stephen would adopt Henry as his heir.

BELOW: The Empress Matilda escapes from Oxford Castle on a snowy night in 1142.

The Norman Legacy

THE NORMAN DYNASTY ENDED with the death of King Stephen in 1154. Henry II, the first Angevin king of England, inherited a country that in some ways resembled England before the conquest: it was a country beset by factions. But throughout the civil war, the administrative system moulded by the first three Norman kings held together. Trade flickered on and craft guilds paid their dues. The great fairs, like St Giles' in Winchester, resumed after a while. The exchequer kept going and taxes were paid. The justice system survived, as courts met to hear pleas. The Church even benefited, through monastic foundations set up by those needing to atone for wartime misdeeds.

The arrival of William, Duke of Normandy across the Channel in 1066 had a dramatic impact on English culture. His conquest, his kingship and his successors left England, and later the rest of Britain, an enduring legacy of language, law and architecture. The Normans gave fresh energy to the Saxon state, adapting law, government, Church and economy to create an efficient, centralized administration that produced the exchequer and the Domesday Book. They built solid castles and splendid cathedrals; they introduced over half the words currently used in the English language; they kept invaders at bay and drew internal borders that still exist today. Above all, William's victory at Hastings wrenched England away from the Scandinavian world and into the mainstream of European history.

ABOVE: Henry II on horseback, depicted on the reverse of his royal seal.

ABOVE: The Norman kings of England, from a history by Matthew Paris (1250–59). Each holds a building with which he was connected: William I, Battle Abbey (top left); William II, Westminster Palace Hall (top right); Henry I, Reading Abbey (bottom left); and Stephen, Faversham Abbey (bottom right).

Places to visit

Battle Abbey, East Sussex: site of the Battle of Hastings.

Bayeux Musem, Bayeux, northern France: Bayeux Tapestry displayed.

Bury St Edmunds, Suffolk: Norman tower gateway and church.

Church of the Holy Sepulchre, Cambridge: rare surviving round church.

Canterbury Cathedral, Kent: Norman crypt with carvings.

Castle Rising, Norfolk: early Norman castle and church.

Chepstow Castle, Monmouthshire.

Chester Cathedral: former Benedictine abbey.

Chichester Cathedral, West Sussex: resemblances to St Stephen's, Caen, church of William I.

Colchester Castle, Essex: Norman keep.

Cormac's Chapel, Cashel, Co. Tipperary, Ireland: Romanesque church.

Dover Castle, Kent.

Dunfermline Abbey, Fife: remains of Benedictine abbey.

Durham Castle and Cathedral: outstanding examples of Norman architecture.

Edinburgh Castle: St Margaret's Chapel.

Ely Cathedral, Cambridgeshire: Norman doorways and carvings.

Exeter Cathedral, Devon: Norman features; Exon Domesday, an early draft of the survey.

Fountains Abbey, Yorkshire: remains of Cistercian monastery.

Gloucester Cathedral: Norman nave and crypt; tomb of Robert Curthose, Duke of Normandy.

Kilpeck Church, Herefordshire: well-preserved church, one of the finest in Britain, noted for its carving.

Lincoln: Norman castle and cathedral (doorways and carvings); Jew's House and other Norman dwellings.

London:
British Museum; Museum of London; Victoria and Albert Museum; Public Records Office, Kew: Domesday Book; Tower of London: White Tower, built by William I and William II; Westminster Abbey: Norman undercroft of dormitory; Westminster Hall, Houses of Parliament: banqueting hall of William Rufus.

Mellifont Abbey,
Co. Louth, Ireland.

Norwich, Norfolk: castle, museum and cathedral; Carrow Abbey; marketplace.

Oxford: castle tower (St George's) and mound; cathedral.

Pembroke Castle, Dyfed.

Peterborough Cathedral, Cambridgeshire: fine example of Romanesque architecture.

Pevensey Castle, East Sussex: Roman fort built on by Normans.

Rochester, Kent: castle and cathedral.

Romsey Abbey, Hampshire: unspoilt Norman church.

Salisbury, Wiltshire: Old Sarum, remains of Norman cathedral's ground plan.

Tewkesbury Abbey, Gloucestershire: Romanesque church, tall columns and central tower.

Weald & Downland Museum, Singleton, West Sussex: reconstructions of domestic buildings.

Winchester, Hampshire: cathedral, early Norman transepts, Norman font; St Cross Hospital Norman church.

Worcester Cathedral: Romanesque crypt; circular chapter house.